Heroes and Heroines of the American Revolution

Peter F. Copeland

DOVER PUBLICATIONS, INC.
Mineola, New York

To Mimi and Ali Shannon—
two rebel girls.

Bibliographical Note

Heroes and Heroines of the American Revolution is a new work, first published by Dover Publications, Inc., in 2004.

International Standard Book Number

ISBN-13: 978-0-486-43324-0
ISBN-10: 0-486-43324-2

Manufactured in the United States by Courier Corporation
43324205
www.doverpublications.com

INTRODUCTION

Lasting from 1775 to 1783, the American Revolution is a significant and far-reaching event in modern history. The origins of Continental dissent grew out of the French and Indian War (1754–1763), in which Britain incurred great costs in the defense of the colonies. To cover the losses, Britain levied a series of taxes on the colonists over the years without allowing them representation in the decision-making proceedings. Growing resentment was fueled by the refusal of Parliament to acknowledge the complaints, and by the continued presence of British troops quartered in the colonies. Finally, confrontation began with the Boston Massacre in 1770, and escalated after the Battle of Lexington and Concord—the first open conflict in the War of Independence.

With the entry of France, Spain, and the Netherlands into the war, the revolution became an international event. Battles raged on land and sea, with the other countries contributing much in terms of capital, munitions, naval forces, and soldiers. The war was essentially over with the surrender of Lord Cornwallis and his 7,000 troops at Yorktown in 1781, but was not officially ended until the Treaty of Paris was signed in 1783.

I have depicted as wide a range of heroes and heroines as space allows, but there are many others—on both sides of the struggle—who also acted courageously in service to their loyalties. In this book, you will find, not only generals and statesmen, but also ordinary soldiers and innovative women whose bravery, suffering, and perseverance are inspiring to all. Many lost their lives in this war, but without their sacrifices, the United States of America would perhaps not be the mighty nation it is today, with a foundation based on ideals of "life, liberty and the pursuit of happiness," as Jefferson wrote so magnificently in the Declaration of Independence.

Thomas Jefferson (1743–1826). An influential Patriot and the new nation's third president, Thomas Jefferson was a champion of freedom from political and religious tyranny. His early revolutionary leanings were apparent in the controversial pamphlet, "A Summary View on the Rights of British America," written in 1774. As a founding member of the Continental Congress, Jefferson drafted the Declaration of Independence in 1776 "to place befo[re] mankind the common sense of the subject, in terms [as] plain and firm as to command their assent." After ser[v]ing as Secretary of State to Washington and Vi[ce] President to Adams, Jefferson was elected President an[d] served two terms before retiring to Monticello, h[is] Virginia home.

PLATE   1

George and Martha Washington. George Washington (1732–1799) was already a veteran soldier when he was chosen by the Continental Congress to command the newly formed Continental Army. A leader in the movement for American independence, Washington was a delegate to the Continental Congress and Commander-in-Chief of its army, which he lead to a difficult but tri-umphant victory against the British. After participating in the Constitutional Convention, the "Father of Our Country" was elected the first President of the United States in 1789 for the first of the two terms. His wife, Martha Custis Washington (1731–1802) was beloved as a gracious hostess, both at the President's House and at the Washingtons' Virginia estate, Mount Vernon.

PLATE 2

John and Abigail Adams. Active in colonial politics in his native Massachusetts, John Adams (1735–1826) was an early advocate of American independence. With a background in law, he served in both Continental Congresses, helped compose the Declaration of Independence, and collaborated on terms of peace with Great Britain to end the Revolutionary War. Adams was the first Vice President of the United States, and its second president. His wife, Abigail (1744–1818), was a prolific correspondent whose letters to her husband offer insight into life in the colonial era, both as a woman and as a Patriot. Their son, John Quincy Adams, became the sixth president of the United States.

PLATE 3

Thayendanegea, aka Joseph Brant (1742–1807). A Mohawk chief and officer in the British military, Joseph Brant allied himself and his people with the British side. If the Patriots were defeated, he hoped his allegiance to the British would secure land for his tribe. He led a number of formidable raids against the colonists in the southern New York region, earning a reputation for fierce combat. Two of his most notable successes were the Battle of Oriskany in 1777, and the Cherry Valley Massacre in 1778. After the war, he brought the Mohawks to a reservation in Ontario, where he performed missionary work and sought to retain land rights on behalf of his people.

PLATE 4

Nathan Hale (1755–1776). Nathan Hale, born in Connecticut, was a schoolteacher until he enrolled in the local militia at the age of twenty. Progressing from lieutenant to captain, Hale saw little action until his appointment as one of Knowlton's Rangers, a division dedicated to reconnaissance and intelligence missions. He was captured by the British in New York in September 1776, arrested as a spy, and was hanged the next day. At his execution, the twenty-one-year-old soldier spoke the words that inspired many of his compatriots: "I regret that I have but one life to lose for my country." Remembered as a martyr, Hale is honored for his dedication to the Patriot cause to this day.

PLATE 5

Deborah Sampson (1760–1827). A Massachusetts native, Deborah Sampson grew up listening to her relatives tell stories of the family's harrowing experiences in the American wilderness after arriving on the Mayflower. At the age of twenty-one, she disguised herself as a man and enlisted in her local militia under the name Robert Shurtleff. She traveled with her regiment and escaped notice until she was wounded in the leg in New York. The military physician soon discovered her ruse and arranged for her to be honorably discharged and sent home.

PLATE 6

Paul Revere (1735–1818). A master goldsmith and silversmith, Revere is most famous for riding from Boston to nearby Lexington to warn fellow Patriots of the British arrival on April 18, 1775. His revolutionary interests grew from his membership in local groups, and he used his community involvement to promote the cause, which he ardently supported. He served as a lieutenant colonel in the Massachusetts militia, though he saw little fighting. At the end of the war, he returned to metalworking including the casting of bells—one of which still toll before each service at Boston's King's Chapel.

PLATE 7

Molly Pitcher (1754–1832). Mary Ludwig Hays was a dedicated army wife whose husband, John Hays, enlisted as a gunner in the Pennsylvania artillery. Following him onto the field at the Battle of Monmouth, she occupied herself toward the comfort of the soldiers—washing, mending, cooking, nursing, and bringing vessels of water to the thirsty men, which earned her the good-natured nickname. According to stories, when her husband collapsed from a wound, Mary Hays courageously took his place at the gun and continued his work at the cannon until the Battle of Monmouth was won. For her heroic actions, the military awarded her a $40 annual pension until her death.

PLATE 8

Marquis de Lafayette (1757–1834). The Marquis de Lafayette was a wealthy French aristocrat who was inspired to come to America and aid the colonists in their struggle for independence. Commissioned a major general by the Continental Congress in 1777, he joined Washington's staff and was tireless in pursuit of the American cause. He returned to France during the war to elicit aid, and was instrumental in forming the military alliance between America and France that ultimately assured the colonies' independence. In 1780, he commanded the Patriot army in defense of Virginia, and was a key player in the siege at Yorktown in Virginia. He later became involved in the revolution in his own country, narrowly escaping with his life.

PLATE 9

Francis Marion (1732–1795). Popularly remembered as the "Swamp Fox" due to his shrewd military tactics, Francis Marion was a captain in the South Carolina militia when his commanding general surrendered to the British in South Carolina in 1780. Marion gathered a band of soldiers and, employing guerrilla tactics, ambushed British regiments in the swamps of his home territory. In 1781, he received a special commendation from Congress after leading a rescue of Patriots that were surrounded by British troops in Parkers Ferry, South Carolina, and was promoted to brigadier general.

PLATE 10

Margaret Cochran Corbin (1751–1800). Born on the frontier, Margaret Cochran married John Corbin in 1775 and accompanied him to battle after he enlisted in the Pennsylvania artillery. With her husband's regiment under attack by Hessian troops, Margaret Corbin watched him get killed at his gunner and took his place to continue the battle. Wounded by grapeshot, she survived the battle but was seriously disabled from her injuries received that day. Congress recognized her contribution and awarded her a half-pension for the remainder of her life. In later years, it was said "Captain Molly" always wore a soldier's coat and smoked a pipe.

Plate 11

Nathanael Greene (1742–1786). Beginning as the Commander of the Rhode Island army, Nathanael Greene quickly ascended the ranks of the Patriot military to become a general and Commander-in-Chief of the southern ranks in 1778. Having fought with Washington in Boston and New York at the start of the war, Greene faced Britain's Lord Cornwallis in South Carolina in 1781. He succeeded in thinning the British ranks to enable American general Daniel Morgan's significant defeat of Cornwallis. Later that year, Greene was instrumental in trapping a section of British forces in Charleston until the Patriots achieved victory in the war.

PLATE   12

Comte de Rochambeau (1725–1807). Jean-Baptiste-Donatien de Vimeur, a brigadier general and governor in France, brought 6,000 soldiers to the colonies in an expeditionary bid to aid the Patriots against the British. Joining his army with that of George Washington in Yorktown, Rochambeau and his Franco-American comrades laid siege to Cornwallis's troops from both land and sea, securing his defeat. This victory for the Patriots was the defining event that ensured the independence of the colonies.

PLATE   13

Betty Zane (ca. 1766–ca. 1831). According to legend, Betty Zane was a courageous sixteen-year-old who lived with her brothers in Wheeling, West Virginia, in a house located close to Fort Henry. When the town was attacked by Indians, the residents took refuge in the fort but failed to bring an adequate amount of gunpowder. Zane volunteered to run to her brothers' house and fetch more powder, insisting that "'tis better a maid than a man should die." The surprised Indians merely watched her exit the fort, but began shooting when they noticed her load of gunpowder upon her return. Zane escaped injury, and her brave mission allowed the townspeople to defeat the Indians successfully.

PLATE 14

George Rogers Clark (1752–1818). A frontier military officer, Clark is remembered as the "Conqueror of the Northwest." Leading a band of less than two hundred soldiers, he defended the Kentucky area from British attack in 1778, and led his men in both the capture of Vincennes and the defense of St. Louis from the British.

His actions were responsible for the award of the Northwest region to America in the Treaty of Paris, which ended the war. Clark and his men received no pay during the war, and even incurred debt over the equipment and supplies they used in battle.

PLATE 15

Phillis Wheatley (1753–1784). The United States' first noted black female poet, Phillis Wheatley was kidnapped from her native Senegal as a child and sold as a slave in Boston to a Quaker family. Observing her interest in learning, the Wheatleys educated the girl in English and classical languages, and cultivated her talent in poetry. Her first book of verse was published in London in 1773, and her subsequent social success enabled her to meet George Washington and Benjamin Franklin. This drawing of Wheatley is copied from an engraved portrait by Scipio Moorhead as it appeared in the frontispiece of her book, *Poems on Various Subjects, Religious and Moral.*

PLATE 16

Ethan Allen (1738–1789). Declared an outlaw over a territorial dispute with New York concerning present-day Vermont, Ethan Allen organized a group of frontiersmen called the "Green Mountain Boys" to terrorize enforcers and settlers in the area under question. With the start of the Revolutionary War, Allen mobilized his men and troops from Connecticut to join the Patriot cause, and seized Fort Ticonderoga from the British in 1775. Later that year, in a doomed attempt to gain control of Montreal, Allen was captured and held prisoner until his release in 1778.

PLATE 17

Nancy Hart (ca. 1735–1830). According to a number of legends, Nancy Hart was a brave wife and mother who lived in a log cabin on the Georgia frontier in the perilous time of war. Stories tell of a day when Loyalists arrived at her doorstep when she and her children were at home, and demanded a meal of her last turkey. While preparing the meal, Hart sent her daughter to summon help while she surreptitiously hid the soldiers' rifles. When the Loyalists noticed her actions, she took up a rifle, shot two of them, and hanged the others with her neighbors' assistance. In some legends, she also worked as a spy for the Georgia militia, gathering information from enemy camps in the area.

PLATE 18

Casimir Pulaski (1747–1779). A distinguished soldier in his native country of Poland, Casimir Pulaski fled to France to avoid the Prussian invasion, and there met Benjamin Franklin, who recommended him to George Washington. Pulaski arrived in the colonies in 1777 and served under Washington before being appointed a general and chief of cavalry by Congress. He fought in key battles at Brandywine, Germantown, and Charleston before being mortally wounded in 1779 at the siege of Savannah.

PLATE 19

Daniel Morgan (1736–1802). At the outbreak of the war, Daniel Morgan assembled his own company of Virginia riflemen and was named captain of the troop. He accompanied Benedict Arnold on the march to Quebec in 1776, and assumed leadership of the soldiers when Arnold was wounded. Though he was captured and held, he was released later that year and participated in the Battle of Saratoga in 1777. He resigned in 1779, but was called from retirement to assist in halting Cornwallis's southerly progress. Promoted to brigadier general, Morgan led his troops to victory at Cowpens, South Carolina, thereby preventing Cornwallis from taking North Carolina.

PLATE 20

Anthony Wayne (1745–1796). A celebrated officer with numerous victories to his credit, "Mad" Anthony Wayne, as he was known, began as a colonel in the Continental Army before being promoted to brigadier general in 1777. He fought at Brandywine, Germantown, and Monmouth, but was most hailed for leading the triumphant seizure of the British fort at Stony Point. Wayne also directed a regiment to Yorktown, where he joined Lafayette in the siege, then traveled south to Georgia to rout British-allied Indians from the region.

PLATE   21

Baron von Steuben (1730–1794). Friedrich Wilhelm von Steuben was a retired captain in the Prussian army when he was recommended to Washington by Benjamin Franklin and Silas Deane, who were in France at the time. Steuben began his colonial military career as a training officer, rigorously molding the inexperienced troops at Valley Forge in the winter of 1777. He wrote the definitive training manual for the army, then was elevated to the rank of major general, with the role as the army's Inspector General. On the field, he held a combat command in Virginia and led a division in the Battle of Yorktown.

PLATE 22

Comte de Grasse (1722–1788). François-Joseph-Paul, comte de Grasse was a French naval officer who led a squadron of ships westward at the outbreak of French involvement in the Revolutionary War. He engaged the British in naval battle in the West Indies, but was summoned to Virginia to aid the Patriots in the decisive Battle of Yorktown. Though attacked by the British upon his arrival at Chesapeake Bay, de Grasse fought the offensive and kept Cornwallis's garrison from retreating through that route. His sailors then joined the battle on land, which ultimately led to Cornwallis's surrender.

PLATE 23

Alexander Hamilton (ca. 1755–1804). An early proponent of the revolution, Alexander Hamilton was a college student when commissioned to be a captain of a regional artillery outfit in New York. In the Battle of Trenton, his troops deflected an attack by Cornwallis on Washington's army. Greatly aided by this action, Washington took Hamilton under his wing as an aide-de-camp. Bored of administrative duties and seeking field action, he left Washington's regiment in 1781 and soon commanded a squadron at Yorktown against the British. With the war nearly over, Hamilton entered law school and was later instrumental in the formation of the new nation's government.

PLATE 24

Benjamin Franklin (1706–1790). A brilliant and versatile man, Benjamin Franklin was well known for his inventions and political involvement when the war began. Though he pressed for a reasonable system of self-governing states under British rule, writing more than 120 articles on the subject, he later recognized the need for revolution and committed himself to the cause. His key role was that of securing an alliance with the French, which ultimately sent almost 50,000 men to aid the colonists in their struggle. He also assisted in the terms of peace to end the war, and served as a delegate in the Continental Congress to help draft the Declaration of Independence.

PLATE 25

Patrick Henry (1736–1799). Born in Virginia, Patrick Henry is remembered as an inspired orator, statesman, and Patriot. He cultivated his speaking skills first as a lawyer, then as an outspoken opponent of British tyranny. When arguing in favor of arming the Virginia military, he spoke his famously inspiring words, "I know not what course others may take, but as for me, give me liberty or give me death." As wartime governor of Virginia, he granted support to George Washington and the Continental army, and was reelected twice by his constituents.

PLATE 26

John Paul Jones (1747–1792). A sailor since his childhood in Scotland, John Paul Jones (originally John Paul—he changed his name to avoid arrest for killing a mutinous crewmember) was a shipmaster when the war broke, and was named a senior lieutenant of the Continental navel force upon his enlistment. After participating in notable skirmishes from the West Indies to the Canadian coast, Jones took command of the

Bonhomme Richard and sailed to the British Isles, where he encountered two larger and better-armed British ships. During the fierce naval battle, Jones heard a call for him to surrender and declared, "I have not yet begun to fight!" Despite heavy casualties and the loss of his vessel, he vanquished the two British ships and sailed them to the Netherlands in triumph.

PLATE 27

Sell your books at
World of Books!
Go to sell.worldofbooks.com
and get an instant price
quote. We even pay the
shipping - see what your old
books are worth today!

Inspected By: Laura_Galindo

0008374 5284

c-2

L-3

Thomas Paine (1737–1809). An influential writer, Thomas Paine emigrated to America from England in 1774, just as Continental dissent was rising. Observing the plight of the colonists, he wrote a fifty-page pamphlet called "Common Sense," which called for the independence of the colonies, and was a foundation for the Declaration of Independence. From 1776–1783, he issued sixteen more pamphlets called "The American Crisis," one of which began with the well-known words, "These are the times that try men's souls." As clerk of the General Assembly of Pennsylvania, he had first-hand knowledge of the lack of pay and supplies for the soldiers, which added to their discontent. He donated a large portion of his salary to this effort, and traveled to France to acquire more money and equipment, which greatly assisted the American cause.

PLATE 28

John Stark (1728–1822). A colonel at the start of the war, John Stark participated in the Battle of Bunker Hill, as well as conflicts in New Jersey and Canada. After leading a victory at the Battle of Bennington, he was promoted to brigadier general in the Continental Army. His troops assisted in the victory of the Battle of Saratoga by blocking the retreat of Britain's General Burgoyne across the Hudson River, leading him to be surrounded by Patriot ranks. This defeat devastated the British and convinced the French to enter the war as an American ally. Stark went on to serve in battles in Rhode Island and New Jersey, and was promoted to major general for his decisive leadership.

PLATE 29

Henry Lee (1756–1818). Nicknamed "Light-horse Harry Lee," Henry Lee was commissioned a captain of the cavalry in 1776, and assembled "Lee's Legion." Made of three troops each of cavalry and infantry, it was one of the most active and efficient military units in the Continental army. Promoted to major in 1770, he surprised the British stronghold at Paulus Hook, New Jersey, taking many prisoners and restoring the morale of the Patriots. As lieutenant colonel, he played an effective role in the southern campaign in 1780–1781. Henry Lee was the father of Robert E. Lee, of Civil War fame.

PLATE   30

Joseph Warren (1741–1775). A respected physician and active Patriot in Massachusetts, Warren was the messenger that gave Paul Revere the urgent news of the British arrival and sent him on the fateful ride to Lexington and Concord. He helped write a series of protest pamphlets called the "Suffolk Resolves," which were addressed to the British Parliament and approved by the Continental Congress. Commissioned a major general in June 1775, Warren joined the Battle of Bunker Hill three days later and was one of the last defenders of the redoubt at Breed's Hill. He was killed during the final hours of the conflict, and is remembered with a monument erected on the place where he fell.

PLATE 31

Nicholas Herkimer (1728–1777). A veteran soldier in the French and Indian War, Nicholas Herkimer was named brigadier general at the start of the revolution. In 1777, with 800 soldiers of the Tryon County militia under his command, Herkimer started for Fort Stanwix near Albany, New York, which was held by colonists and under attack by Loyalists and Indians. During the march, his company was ambushed by a legion of 1,200 British troops in what was to be known as the Battle of Oriskany. When wounded in the leg, Herkimer is said to have continued giving commands while sitting under a tree and smoking a pipe. Both sides suffered heavy losses in the battle, and Herkimer died from complications from his wound days later.

PLATE 32

Henry Knox (1750–1806). A bookstore owner previous to the war, Henry Knox joined the colonial militia in Boston at the outbreak, then enlisted in the Continental Army as a colonel in charge of the artillery. In the winter of 1775, he won praise for transporting six tons of artillery from New York's Fort Ticonderoga to Boston, where it was used to siege the city and drive out the British. Knox was later promoted to brigadier general, and commanded forces at West Point, Monmouth, and Yorktown. He was named Commander-in-Chief of the Continental Army upon Washington's retirement after the war, and became the nation's first Secretary of War in 1789.

PLATE 33

John Glover (1732–1797). An officer in the local militia in Marblehead, Massachusetts, before the war, John Glover reorganized his regiment when the revolution began. One of his first assignments was to find and outfit two naval vessels for use as Washington's fleet. In 1776, he coordinated the stealthy nighttime retreat of the Patriot forces from Long Island, shipping 9,000 men, with their horses and arms, on boats to present-day Manhattan. In December of that year, his regiment also ferried Washington's troops across the Delaware River in a surprise attack on the Hessians in Trenton, New Jersey, which inspired the famous Gilbert Stuart painting of Washington's crossing.

PLATE 34

William Smallwood (1732–1792). Though educated in England and a soldier in the British army, American-born William Smallwood stayed true to his heritage and supported the Patriot cause. Appointed colonel of the Maryland battalion, he led his troops from battle to battle, engaging in conflicts at Brooklyn Heights, White Plains (where he was wounded), Fort Washington, Germantown, and Camden. Winning praise from Congress, Smallwood was named major general of the army, but he refused to serve under General von Steuben due to rank issues. Instead, he returned to Maryland, and later served as governor and a member of Congress.

PLATE 35

Joseph Plumb Martin (ca. 1761–?). Under sixteen years of age when he enlisted in the Continental Army, Joseph Plumb Martin intended to serve for six months to decide if he enjoyed the soldier's life. Instead, he stayed in the army for seven years, during which he participated in a number of key battles, including Long Island, White Plains, Germantown, Monmoth, and Yorktown. Perhaps his greatest contribution was a diary of his experiences as a soldier, including all the amusements and hardships of day-to-day life as a private and Patriot. His humorous and insightful book, *A Narrative of Some of the Adventures, Dangers, and Sufferings of a Revolutionary Soldier,* serves as a valuable historical account and is still read today.

PLATE 36

John Sullivan (1740–1795). A distinguished leader in the Continental Army, John Sullivan first served as brigadier general, then as major general in the revolution. He directed the retreat of the Patriot troops after the Battle of Quebec, then fought in the battle at Long Island, where he was captured and held for several months. He was released during a prisoner exchange, and went on to assist Washington attack Trenton in 1776. Three years later, he notably led troops on an expedition to rout Indians and Loyalists from their homes in northern New York, where they had been attacking Patriots in raids encouraged by the British.

PLATE 37

Sybil Ludington (1761–1839). Sybil Ludington was only sixteen years old when news reached her home of a British advance on nearby Danbury, where the militia's ammunition was stored. The daughter of a Connecticut militia officer, she learned that the Patriot garrison at Danbury was outnumbered and needed reinforcements, and volunteered to ride the countryside and raise the call for other militia outfits. Though unfamiliar with the roads, she traveled forty miles on horseback through Connecticut and New York, alerting the countryside. Thanks to her efforts, more soldiers arrived at Danbury and turned back the British force, thus saving the valuable store of arms.

PLATE 38

Benedict Arnold (1741–1801). Though forever remembered as a traitor to the Patriot cause, Benedict Arnold began as a respected military officer in the Continental Army. He bravely led troops in the battles of Quebec, Valcour Island, Fort Stanwix, and Saratoga, and was highly regarded by George Washington. In 1779, Arnold felt that he was not accorded the proper rank and honor due him, and secretly became an informant to the British of his activities as an Continental general. When his betrayal was discovered, Arnold fled to Britain, where he was resented for leaving behind his British contact to be executed by the Americans. Disliked by both nations, he remained in Britain until his death, when legend claims that he requested his wife to bury him in his blue Continental uniform, asking that God forgive him for ever having put on another.

PLATE 39

Cato Varnum (birth and death unknown). Though not considered a typical hero, Cato Varnum was a sixteen-year-old African-American youth who, in March 1778, enlisted in the 1st Rhode Island Regiment and served to the end of the war. He participated in the siege of Yorktown, where he was a member of the light infantry unit. Despite his youth, his bravery and dedication to the Patriot cause are a true cause of inspiration. This drawing is rendered from a sketch of a black soldier of the Rhode Island Regiment, done by a French officer on the battlefield of Yorktown.

PLATE 40

Abraham Nimham (?–1777). Abraham Nimham, member of the Wappinger tribe in the Stockbridge, Massachusetts area, enlisted himself and his tribesmen as scouts for the Continental army in 1777. Though it is not clear if all of the Stockbridge Indians (which included those from Wappinger and Mohican tribes) were put in one regiment, there were several dozen placed under Captain Nimham's command. He and his fifty-man troop fought in the battles at White Plains, Monmouth, and Barren Hill, before being ambushed by a force of 500 Loyalist and Hessian soldiers at Kingsbridge in New York. The attack destroyed the Patriot regiment, resulting in more than thirty deaths, including Nimham and his father. After the battle, Washington acknowledged the contribution of the Stockbridge Indians, who continued to support the revolution with enlistments.

PLATE 41

Crispus Attucks (ca. 1723–1770). Born of either African or Indian/African ancestry, Crispus Attucks was a fugitive slave who escaped from his master and worked for some years as a merchant seaman. On March 5, 1770, he was one of many colonists who had been inspired by the urgings of Samuel Adams to demonstrate against British troops quartering in Boston. Forming a crowd, they jeered and threw rocks at a group of soldiers, who responded to the attack with gunfire, killing five. Thus, Attucks (the first to fall), Samuel Gray, Samuel Maverick, James Caldwell, and Patrick Carr were the first casualties of the revolution. The Boston Massacre, as it was called, was afteward widely used as an example of British mistreatment. Attucks' body was lain in the city's Faneuil Hall for several days before being buried with the bodies of the other victims.

PLATE 42

Signing the Declaration of Independence. On July 2, 1776, in the midst of the Revolutionary War, the Continental Congress passed a resolution calling for the independence of the thirteen united colonies. Two days later, the Declaration of Independence, drafted mainly by Thoma Jefferson between June 11 and June 28 of that year, wa adopted. On July 9, it was formally signed by the dele gates of the Continental Congress.

PLATE 43

Though the Declaration was adopted, the War of Independence did not end until September 3, 1783. On that date, the Treaty of Paris, which recognized the liberty of the colonies from its former ruler, was signed by representatives of Great Britain and the newly formed nation, the United States of America.

PLATE 44